WONDERS
OF THE WORLD

Caves

Rachel Lynette

WITHDRAWN

KIDHAVEN PRESS

An imprint of Thomson Gale, a part of The Thomson Corporation

THOMSON

GALE

Detroit • New York • San Francisco • San Diego • New Haven, Conn. • Waterville, Maine • London • Munich

THOMSON

---✦---™

GALE

LIBRARY OF CONGRESS CATALOGING-IN-PUBLICATION DATA

Lynette, Rachel.
  Caves / by Rachel Lynette.
    p. cm. — (Wonders of the world)
  Includes bibliographical references and index.
  ISBN 0-7377-2645-8 (alk. paper)
1. Caves—Juvenile literature. I. Title. II. Wonders of the world
(KidHaven Press)
  GB601.2L96 2005
  551.44'7—dc22

                                                    2004024473

Printed in the United States of America

CONTENTS

How Caves Form

Caves are mysterious places. Under the surface of the Earth is a hidden world of narrow passages, giant chambers, and underground lakes, streams, and even waterfalls. Caves are full of secrets. Beautiful rock formations, prehistoric drawings, stolen treasures, and even human remains have all been found in caves. Caves are full of life. There are animals that live in caves that have never seen the light of day. Many kinds of bats make their homes in caves. Caves are wild places. Although many caves have been explored, thousands of miles of caves have never been seen by human eyes.

There are caves on every continent of the world as well as under the ocean. There are more than 40,000 known caves in the United States. Most of these are wild caves, meaning they are not open to the public and may not have been explored. Show caves are public caves where visitors follow lighted passages and often take guided tours.

Waterfalls like this one are among the many wonders that exist inside caves.

A cave or cavern is any natural passage in the earth with an opening to the surface. Caves come in all shapes and sizes. Some are so small that a person could barely fit inside. Others are huge sprawling mazes of passages, some of which open into large rooms. The Mammoth Cave in Kentucky is the biggest network of caves in the world, with more than 360 miles (580km) of underground rooms and passages.

The Mammoth Cave is made up of **solution caves**. Solution caves are the biggest and most common kinds of caves. Three other common types of caves are **sea caves**, **sandstone caves**, and **lava tubes**.

Famous Caves Around the World

Lechuguilla,
USA

Cueva de Infiernillo,
MEXICO

Lascaux,
FRANCE

Sea Caves

Sea caves are formed when powerful ocean waves crash into cliffs along the coastline. Over time the waves erode, or wear away, part of the cliff. Weaker sections of the cliff break off. Slowly a cave forms, getting bigger and bigger until the back of the cave is no longer within the tide's reach.

Most sea caves are full of life. Tide pools inside the caves are alive with starfish, sea anemones, crabs, and small fish. Larger animals such as seals and sea lions find shelter within these caves. There are many sea caves along the

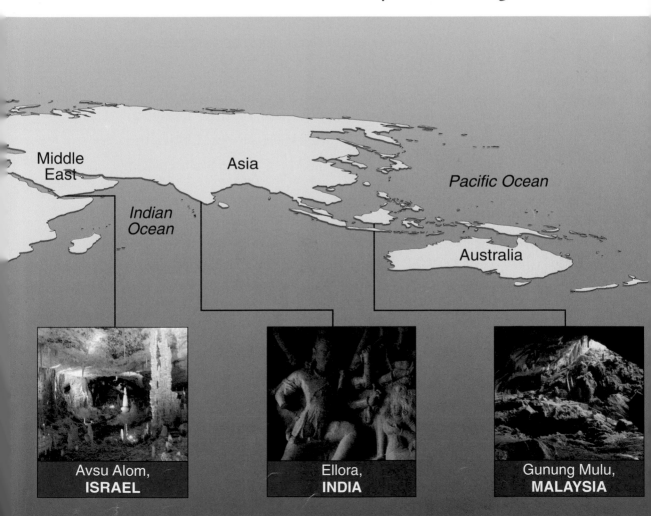

Avsu Alom,
ISRAEL

Ellora,
INDIA

Gunung Mulu,
MALAYSIA

Pacific coast of the United States. Some of the biggest and most famous sea caves are the Sea Lion Caves in Oregon.

Sandstone Caves

Sandstone caves are another type of cave. Sandstone is formed when tiny grains of sand are cemented together by a natural substance such as clay or silica over millions of years. Sandstone is very soft and can be easily eroded by water and wind. Sandstone caves are formed when rivers run down the side of a sandstone cliff, eroding the natural cement and washing away some of the sand. Wind may also add to the process. After many years of erosion, a large, shallow cave is formed. Often these caves are located near the tops of the cliffs, hundreds of feet above the ground.

Many interesting sandstone caves can be found in the southwestern states. Ancient peoples made their homes in these caves, and the ruins can still be seen today. One of the best places to see these ruins is in Mesa Verde State Park in Colorado.

Lava Tubes

Rather than being formed by wind and rain, lava tubes form when volcanoes erupt. Molten lava flows down the side of the volcano. The lava on the surface begins to cool and harden before the lava underneath cools, because it is exposed to the air. The hardened lava on the outside creates a tunnel for the still-molten lava inside to flow through. The lava inside eventually flows out, and a long, hollow tube is left. Lava tubes usually look like the inside of a tunnel or subway.

Sandstone Cave

Sea Cave

Lava Tube

Solution Cave

Lava tubes can be found in the western United States and in Hawaii. One of the longest lava tubes in the world is Ape Cave in Washington. It is nearly 2.5 miles (4km) long and was formed when Mount St. Helens erupted nearly 2,000 years ago.

Strange cave decorations, like this one in New Mexico's Carlsbad Caverns, take thousands of years to form.

Solution Caves

Unlike lava tubes, solution caves form when rainwater mixes with **carbon dioxide** to dissolve large portions of rock. These caves may be made of marble, gypsum, or dolomite, but the biggest and most famous solution caves are made of limestone. Some of the deepest and most interesting limestone caves in the United States are part of Carlsbad Caverns National Park in New Mexico. These caves also contain one of the biggest chambers in the world. The Big Room at Carlsbad Caverns is more than twenty stories high and as big as six football fields. Like other limestone caves, Carlsbad Caverns formed over millions of years.

Limestone actually formed at the bottom of the sea. Millions of years ago most of the Earth was covered with water. Microscopic organisms lived in the water. When these tiny creatures died, their skeletons, which are made from a mineral called **calcite**, sank to the bottom of the ocean. Slowly the ocean floor was covered with a thick layer of calcite skeletons. The skeletons were compressed as more skeletons were piled on top of them and the water weighed down on them. Other minerals in the sea helped cement the calcite skeletons together. After millions of years the calcite hardened into limestone.

In some areas of the world, powerful earthquakes forced the limestone up and out of the water. In other areas the level of the water dropped over time, exposing the limestone. Over the years layers of other kinds of rocks and soil formed on top of the limestone. Plants grew in the soil. Limestone, soil, and plant life were all important ingredients in the process of forming a cave. Only one more thing was needed: rain.

When rainwater seeps into the soil, it absorbs carbon dioxide from the plants in that soil. The carbon dioxide changes the rainwater into a weak acid called **carbonic acid**. The carbonic acid soaks through the soil to the limestone below. It seeps into cracks in the limestone and very slowly dissolves it, making the cracks bigger. Pools of carbonic acid form in the ever-widening cracks. Over millions of years the limestone dissolves away to form the passages and chambers of a cave. Eventually, air finds its way into the cave. When this happens, a lot of the carbon dioxide in the water escapes into the air. The water in the cave is no longer acidic enough to dissolve the limestone, and the cave stops growing.

Even when a cave stops growing, it does not stop changing. Inside many caves are strange and beautiful rock formations. These formations, called cave decorations, are often fragile and take thousands of years to form. Solution caves often have more cave decorations than other types of caves.

CHAPTER TWO

Cave Decorations

The rooms and passages of a cave are filled with decorations of different shapes, sizes, and even colors. Like the cave itself, the decorations are formed by water. This water contains calcite from its journey through the layers of rock above the cave. As the water drips, dribbles, and flows through the cave, it leaves the calcite behind to form these beautiful decorations. If there is only calcite in the water, the formations will be pure white. If there are other minerals in the water, such as iron or manganese, the formations may be shades of gray, brown, yellow, orange, or red. Cave decorations form slowly, over thousands and even millions of years.

A single cave might be studded with thousands of cave decorations, or **speleothems**. A speleothem is any formation created when water deposits minerals in a cave. The word *speleothem* means "cave deposit." **Stalactites,**

stalagmites, soda straws, draperies, popcorn, and pearls are just some of these formations.

Stalactites and Stalagmites

Stalactites are some of the most common cave decorations. Stalactites are carrot-shaped formations that hang from the ceiling of a cave. Stalactites are formed slowly by

This stalagmite formed inside an ancient clay pot found on the floor of a cave in South America.

Dripping water forms tubes called soda straws which can become stalactites.

drops of water. When a drop of water falls from the ceiling of a cave, it leaves a tiny ring of calcite behind. The next drop adds another ring on top of the first one. The drips continue until a fragile tube called a soda straw forms. Many soda straws break before they become stalactites. If a soda straw does not break, it will become a stalactite when the calcite in the water clogs the hole at the bottom of the tube. When this happens, the water starts to flow on the outside of the formation, rather than on the inside. This causes the soda straw to broaden at the top, taking on the carrot or icicle shape that most stalactites have.

Stalactites grow at different rates. If the water is heavy with calcite and dripping quickly, a stalactite might grow at the rate of half an inch (1.25cm) a year. If it is a very slow drip, the stalactite could take as long as a thousand years to grow a single inch (2.5cm). The largest stalactite in the world is in Ireland. It is nearly 22 feet (6.7m) long.

Stalagmites form on the ground, just under stalactites. A stalagmite is formed from the drops of water that fall from stalactites. Although the water has left some calcite on the ceiling, it still holds some. This is deposited on the ground to form a stalagmite. Stalagmites generally have a wide base because the drop spreads out as it splashes on the ground. Many stalagmites have a bowl-shaped indent at the top called a splash cup.

Sometimes stalactites and stalagmites meet. When this happens the result is called a column. Instead of dripping, the water now flows down outside of the column, causing it to get thicker and thicker. Some of the largest columns known are more than 100 feet (30m) tall and 33 feet (10m) around.

Flowstone and Draperies

Water does not always drip to create cave formations. Sometimes it flows along ceilings or walls. This can form flowstones and draperies.

Flowstone formations are always found on the walls of a cave. They are often quite thick. When water flows or seeps down a wall, it leaves a layer of calcite behind. As water continues to flow down the same wall, many layers of calcite build up. The result often looks like a waterfall made of stone.

When stalactites and stalagmites meet, they form thick columns like these.

Draperies are created when drops of water run down a slanted ceiling, leaving behind a trail of calcite. The deposited calcite often looks like the folds of draperies. Draperies can be several feet long and might be only a few inches thick. Draperies usually hang straight down. If there is a steady wind in the cave, however, they grow to look as if they are blowing in the wind.

Other Cave Decorations

Other cave decorations include rimstone dams, popcorn, and pearls. Rimstone dams are small walls of calcite that surround shallow pools of water. Often, rimstone dams form terraces, with one pool above another and water overflowing to the lower pool. Geologists are not sure how these dams form. One theory is that these pools of water sometimes get overloaded with calcite. The extra

Flowstone formations are thick layers of calcite found on the walls of caves.

This calcite deposit that looks like a curtain hanging from the cave ceiling is known as a drapery.

calcite runs toward the edges of the pools, where it forms the dams.

Popcorn is one of the more common cave formations. It forms when calcite deposits in small knobby bumps along the walls of a cave. Pearls are much more unusual. Cave pearls can be less than 1 inch (2.5cm) or as big as 4 inches

Cave Decorations

Gypsum
Chandeliers

Translucent
Orange Stalactites

Calcite
Cave Pearls

Aragonite–Tipped
Soda Straw

Gypsum Flowers

(10cm) in diameter. Smaller pearls have a round shape, while larger ones tend to have an irregular shape. Cave pearls form in shallow pools or under dripping water. Just like a pearl inside an oyster, cave pearls begin with a grain of sand or small piece of speleothem. Calcite is slowly deposited around the center until the pearl forms. The dripping water not only deposits the calcite but also moves the pearl around so that it is covered evenly to form the round shape. Unlike other cave decorations, cave pearls are not attached to the cave. Although people should never take them, this makes them easy for people to steal. This may be one reason they are so rare.

Damaged Decorations

Unfortunately, people do much more damage to cave decorations than stealing cave pearls. Early explorers and tourists were careless, damaging the fragile cave formations with every step. Many broke off stalactites to take as souvenirs. Early cave explorers sometimes broke stalactites to mark their trail, so they could find their way back to the cave entrance. Even gently touching the formations can harm them. The oils from people's skin can discolor the stone and, if the formation is still growing, can repel the dripping water, halting the formation's growth.

Today most people know that cave decorations are fragile and can take thousands or even millions of years to grow. They treat caves with respect and are careful not to touch any of the formations. The chance to see so many beautiful formations is just one of the things that attracts people to caves. Caves also hold many living mysteries.

CHAPTER THREE

Cave Life

Animals have lived in caves for thousands, perhaps millions of years. Cave explorers have found the bones of many kinds of animals. Some of these bones are thousands of years old. Some of the oldest bones are from prehistoric animals that are now extinct. Most of these bones, however, are from animals that have died recently.

Caves are home to a surprising number of animal species. Animals may live in pools and streams running through caves, in nooks and crannies, under rocks, or even on the ceiling. The animals that live in caves can be divided into three groups, according to how much time they spend in the cave.

Trogloxenes

Trogloxenes are animals that spend only part of their lives in caves. The word *trogloxene* means "cave guest." These animals use the cave for shelter, hibernation, or as a safe place to raise their babies. Most of them spend their time in the entrance area of the cave, where sunlight reaches. They may sometimes venture into the twilight area of the cave. This is the section of cave between the entrance and the part that is completely dark. The twilight area provides a protected place for animals to hide but still allows them to see what is around them. These animals rarely spend time in the dark parts of the cave where they cannot see anything at all. Trogloxenes include bears, bobcats, porcupines, pack rats, raccoons, skunks, moths, mosquitoes, and sometimes, humans.

Bats are the best-known trogloxenes. Unlike other trogloxenes, bats spend most of their time in the dark part

Bats, the most common trogloxenes, sleep in caves during the day and hunt for food at night.

of the cave. This is because bats are nocturnal mammals, which means they sleep during the day and are awake at night. Caves provide bats with a dark, protected place to sleep and a place to hibernate during the winter months. A cave may be home to just a few bats or a million bats. Carlsbad Caverns has one of the biggest bat colonies. More than 1 million Mexican freetail bats live there. Hundreds of tourists come each evening to watch these bats leave the caves. It can take more than two hours for all the bats to fly out of the cave. From a distance, the bats look like a giant cloud of smoke.

Bats leave their caves to hunt. Most bats eat insects. A bat will eat half its weight in insects each night. In the

Mexican freetail bats leave their cave at dusk in search of insects to eat.

southern states there are millions of bats. It is estimated that these bats eat more than 100,000 tons (90,000 metric tons) of insects each year. Without the bats, this area of the country would be overrun with insects!

Bats spend most of their time in caves hanging from the ceiling by their toes. They often crowd together, making it look as if the ceiling is covered with a thick, brown rug. All those bats create a huge amount of droppings. Bat droppings are called **guano**. In some of the rooms in Carlsbad Caverns, people have found layers of guano more than 36 feet (12m) deep! Guano is made of the insects that bats eat. These droppings are an important source of food for other animals that live in the cave.

Troglophiles

Troglophiles are animals that like the dark, moist environment of a cave. The word *troglophile* means "cave lover." Troglophiles may live their entire lives in caves, but they do not have to live in a cave to survive. They can also live in other dark, moist places such as under rocks. Troglophiles spend most of their time in the dark or twilight parts of the cave. Some troglophiles leave the cave at night to find food, while others never do this. Troglophiles include some kinds of beetles, salamanders, frogs, snails, crickets, millipedes, worms, daddy longlegs, and spiders.

Troglobites

Another variety of cave animals is the **troglobites**. *Troglobite* means "cave life." Animals in this group live their entire lives in the dark part of a cave and cannot survive

Cave Animals

Bat

Bear

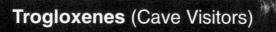

Trogloxenes (Cave Visitors)

Racoon

Bobcat

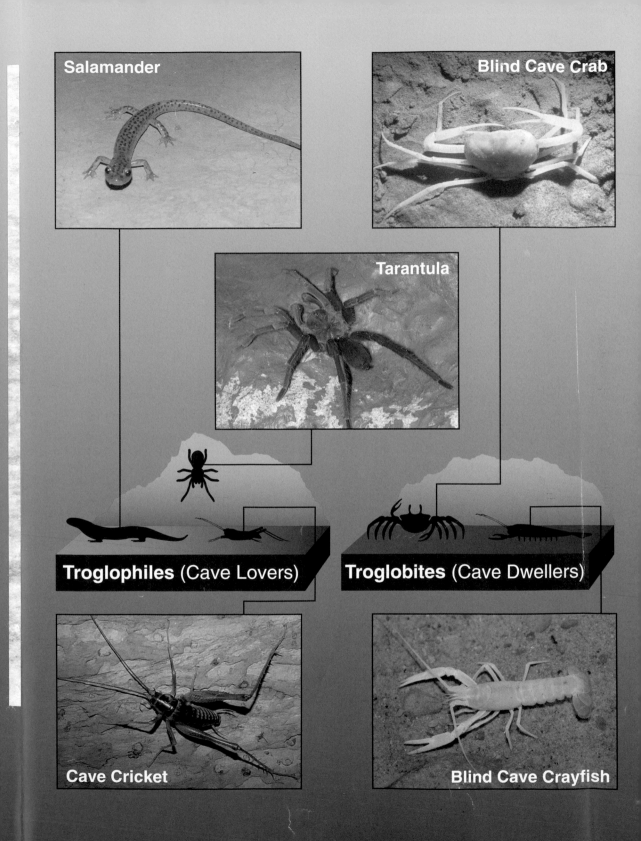

Salamander

Blind Cave Crab

Tarantula

Troglophiles (Cave Lovers)

Troglobites (Cave Dwellers)

Cave Cricket

Blind Cave Crayfish

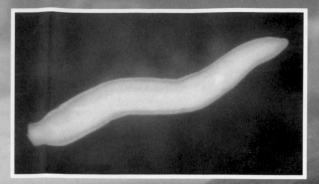

Spending their entire lives in the dark part of a cave, flatworms (inset) are one of the world's oldest troglobites. This species of salamander (above), also a troglobite, breathes through the gills on its neck.

outside the cave. These animals never see the sun or feel its warmth. They have adapted to the cave environment over many years. They are all blind, and some do not even have eyes. After all, they do not need eyes, because there is no light in the dark part of a cave. Most troglobites are white or pink. Many have thin, nearly see-through skin, because they do not need protection from the Sun. Most have long legs or feelers to help them find their way in the dark.

One of the oldest kinds of troglobites are flatworms. Flatworms are white and only about 1 inch (2.5cm) long.

Flatworms live in water. They are able to cling to rocks and pebbles or may float in a cave pond or stream. Flatworms can regrow parts that are missing. If a flatworm is cut in half, both parts will regrow until there are two whole flatworms. Flatworms feed on animals that fall into the water. Hundreds of flatworms can feed on a single bat.

Unlike flatworms, most small troglobites feed on the fungi and bacteria that live in cave soil. They may also feed on bat guano that a stream or another animal carries to the deeper part of a cave. Some kinds of insects, spiders, millipedes, and crustaceans are troglobites. These creatures along, with other small troglobites, provide food for bigger troglobites that live in the dark parts of caves. These bigger troglobites include some types of fish and salamanders.

Cave Fish and Salamanders

Like all troglobites, cave fish are not very big. Cave fish are thin and no longer than 4 inches (10cm). Cave fish move through the water with a gliding motion. Although they are blind, they are able to sense vibrations in the water using nerves along their head and sides. Sensing these vibrations helps them to swim without bumping into anything and to find food. Although adult cave fish have no known predators, young cave fish are always in danger of being eaten by other cave fish. A baby cave fish could even get eaten by its own parent!

Scientists have discovered nine species of salamanders that are troglobites. These salamanders are smaller and slower than salamanders that live outside of caves.

Some of these species spend most of their lives in the water and breathe through gills on their necks. Other species breathe through their skin. Like cave fish, these salamanders use vibrations to sense other animals and to catch their prey.

Scientists and tourists are fascinated by cave animals. Explorers have also found them interesting, but they can make exploring a cave difficult. Explorers must be careful not to disturb the animals' fragile environment. In addition, it is not easy or pleasant to crawl through several feet of slimy, smelly bat guano!

CHAPTER FOUR

Explorations into the Dark

Exploring a cave can be fun and exciting, but it can also be dangerous. Experienced cave explorers are called **cavers**. Cavers know that to explore a cave safely, they must be in good physical condition, have the right equipment, and know a lot about cave safety.

Cave Explorers

People who explore caves must be in good physical condition because caving can be a lot of work! Passages in a cave can be long and narrow. Sometimes cavers have to hike long distances, squeeze through small spaces, or crawl on their bellies. Most caves also contain a lot of water. Wet rocks can be slippery to walk on. If the water is deep, a caver may need to wade or swim.

Cavers need the right clothing and equipment for their work. Most caves range between 55 and 65°F (13 and

Cavers sometimes have to use rope to lower themselves hundreds of feet to a cave's floor.

18°C). Cavers need warm clothing and good boots. Limestone is hard and can cause serious injury, so cavers must protect their heads by wearing helmets. Most cavers wear helmets with a light on the front. A caver should have two other sources of light as well. Other equipment a caver might need includes heavy gloves, knee and elbow pads, ropes and climbing equipment, a first-aid kit, and a whistle. The most important thing a caver needs is friends. A person should never explore a cave alone. Cavers should always explore in groups of three or more.

Cavers must also know how to keep themselves safe while they are exploring caves. Experienced cavers always tell someone where they are caving and when they are going to return. They know how to explore a cave without getting lost. If cavers do lose their way, they know to stay in one place and wait for rescuers. Although there is often a lot of

Emergency workers enter a cave in search of cavers stranded inside.

water in a cave, it should not be drunk. Cavers need to bring plenty of water as well as high-energy food. In addition, cavers must know how to explore the cave without harming any of the cave life or cave formations.

Sometimes cavers discover interesting artifacts or treasure. Even discovering a cave itself can be an adventure. Twenty-four-year-old Elijah Davidson nearly lost his life when he discovered the Oregon Caves.

The Oregon Caves Discovery

Like most caves in the United States, the Oregon Caves were probably discovered by Native Americans long before Europeans ever set foot in the New World. The first recorded discovery of the caves happened in 1874 when Davidson was hunting with his dog, Bruno. Bruno was chasing a bear, and the bear ran into the cave. Davidson did not want to lose his dog, so he followed him. Davidson's only source of light was some matches he had with him. Davidson managed to get pretty far into the cave before he ran out of matches. When he did, he found himself in total darkness.

Davidson could have died in the cave, but he was lucky. He heard the sound of a gurgling stream and found his way to it. He followed the river downstream until he came to the entrance of the cave. Eventually, his dog found his way out too.

Today the Oregon Caves that Davidson discovered are a national monument. Although the cave is not as large as many other show caves, it is unusual because it is carved from marble rather than the more common limestone.

These visitors to Mammoth Cave in the late nineteenth century explored the cave's passages and caverns by boat.

Exploring Mammoth Cave

The Mammoth Cave in Kentucky are the longest network of caves in the world. There are more than 350 miles (563km) of mapped passages, and more are still being discovered. People who visit the caves today can choose from several different guided tours. In the early 1800s, however, almost everyone who visited the caves was guided by an African American slave named Stephen Bishop.

Bishop was just seventeen years old when he began giving tours of the caves. Both tourists and scientists were impressed with his intelligence, knowledge, and enthusiasm. Because of Bishop, the Mammoth Cave soon became a popular tourist attraction.

A caver uses special equipment to collect samples of microbes living in cave pools.

Bishop spent most of his spare time exploring the cave and is credited with many discoveries, including artifacts from prehistoric people and miles of unexplored passages and caverns. One of Bishop's most important discoveries was the first river to be found in Mammoth Cave.

Bishop discovered the river when he was guiding a tourist named H.C. Stevenson. Stevenson wanted to go into parts of the cave that had not yet been explored. Bishop took him to a passageway that was blocked by a deep hole called the Bottomless Pit. It was so deep, they could not see the bottom of it even with their oil lamps. When they dropped a stone into it, it took two and a half seconds to hit the bottom. Stevenson bridged the 6 foot (2m) pit with a cedar-pole ladder, and both men crawled over the rickety bridge to reach the other side. The men then jumped a smaller pit before going down a passage so small they had to stoop to get through. The passage led to the edge of a canyon. At the bottom of the canyon was a large river that together they named the River Styx.

Cave explorers are not always looking for new caves and passages. Sometimes they are interested in what lives inside the cave. Lechuguilla Cave in New Mexico is the deepest cave in the United States and has many beautiful cave formations. The microscopic life inside the cave has made a caver out of National Aeronautics and Space Administration (NASA) biologist Penny Boston.

Lechuguilla Cave and Life on Mars

For a long time people thought that Lechuguilla Cave was a small, unimportant cave. But in 1986, after a lot of rubble was removed, a narrow passage was discovered at the back of the cave. The passage led to a cave system far larger and more spectacular than nearby Carlsbad Caverns. So far more than 100 miles (161km) of passages and rooms have been mapped. What makes the cave important to NASA is that, until recently, it had been cut off from the surface for 2 million years or more. The microscopic creatures, or microbes, that live in the cave have evolved completely isolated from life on the surface.

Boston and her colleagues believe that the environment in Lechuguilla Cave could be similar to what lies under the surface of Mars. They believe that if life can exist deep under the surface of the Earth in Lechuguilla Cave, then similar life-forms could exist on Mars.

One of the reasons these microbes are so fascinating is the way they get their energy. Plants get energy from the Sun. Animals get energy by eating plants or other animals. There is no sunlight in the cave, nor are there plants or animals. Scientists believe that these microbes survive by getting their energy from the minerals in the cave. In other words, they eat rocks.

Boston and the other scientists on her team had to learn a lot about caving before they could go down into the cave. For each expedition they must be lowered 150 feet (43m) down a narrow shaft to the cave floor. Each member of the party has to carry a 50-pound (23kg) backpack full of food, camping supplies, and scientific equipment. The cave is full of mud, dirt, and rocks, and there is plenty of hiking and crawling to do before cavers can get to a large room where they can set up a base camp.

Clues to Life on Other Planets

The scientists look for walls covered with brown slime. The microbes they are searching for create the slime. The scientists take samples of the microbes to learn more about them. They hope that learning about these microbes will give them important clues about what to look for on Mars.

Microbes found in New Mexico's Lechuguilla Cave (pictured) could be similar to life-forms on Mars.

Caves are fascinating places. Tourists can visit show caves to learn more about cave life and cave formations. Cavers can find adventure exploring the underground passages and rooms of wild caves. Scientists can learn about geology, cave life, and maybe even other planets.

Glossary

calcite: The main mineral in limestone formed over millions of years from the skeletons of microscopic sea creatures.

carbon dioxide: A gas composed of carbon and oxygen.

carbonic acid: An acid formed when rainwater picks up carbon dioxide from the soil.

cavers: People who explore caves.

guano: Bat droppings.

lava tubes: Caves formed near volcanoes as hot lava cools on the surface and the lava underneath flows away.

sandstone caves: Caves formed by wind as it blows away particles of sand from sandstone cliffs.

sea caves: Caves formed at the bottom of cliffs by ocean waves that beat against the cliffs, wearing through them and breaking away pieces of rock.

solution caves: Caves formed over thousands or millions of years as water that contains carbonic acid dissolves the limestone beneath the surface of the Earth, forming rooms and passages.

speleothems: Cave decorations such as stalactites and stalagmites formed when mineral-rich water is deposited in a cave.

stalactites: Common calcite formations that hang from the ceiling of a cave. Most are carrot shaped.

stalagmites: Common calcite formations on the floor of caves directly below a stalactite.

troglobites: Animals that can live only in the dark area of a cave.

troglophiles: An animal that can live in the dark area of a cave but can also live in dark environments outside a cave, such as under a rock or log.

trogloxenes: Animals that spend part of their lives in caves to sleep, hibernate, or raise their young but must look outside the cave for food.

For Further Exploration

Books

Nancy Holler Aulenbach and Hazel A. Barton, *Exploring Caves: Journeys into the Earth*. Washington, DC: National Geographic Society, 2001. This book follows the authors, who are expert cavers, as they explore three very different caves. It features engaging, informative text and beautiful photos as well as a map and glossary. This book is a companion to the IMAX movie *Journey into Amazing Caves*.

Jackie Gaff, *I Wonder Why Stalactites Hang Down and Other Questions About Caves*. Boston: Kingfisher, 2003. This appealing and informative book answers many questions that children have about caves. Includes interesting facts and great colorful pictures.

Roy A. Gallant, *Limestone Caves*. New York: Franklin Watts, 1998. This is an informative book that includes chapters on cave formation, cave life, and cave art. It also has a glossary.

Chris Howe, *Caving*. Chicago: Heinemann, 2003. This book from the Radical Sports series gives the reader information on how to cave. Includes sections on mapping and cave safety as well as an overview of international caving.

G. Thomas Rea, *Caving Basics: A Comprehensive Guide for Beginning Cavers*. Huntsville, AL: National Speleological

Society, 1992. This book is packed with information about caving. There are sections on equipment, safety, maps, geology, and more. This book should be read with an adult to learn about exploring caves safely.

Web Sites

Cave of the Winds Kid's Page (www.caveofthewinds. com/test/kidpage.html). This Web site features some cave activities just for kids. The site includes fun quizzes, a science project, a maze, and other puzzles.

Cave Stories (www.jamesmdeem.com/stories.cave.htm). This Web site features three exciting and true cave stories by children's author James M. Deem.

Lechuguilla Photo Map (www.resurgentsoftware.com/ Lech.html). This clickable map of recently discovered Lechuguilla Cave allows the user to view beautiful photographs of some of the most spectacular cave formations in the world.

Mammoth Cave National Park (www.nps.gov/maca). This is the official Web site for Mammoth Cave in Kentucky, which is the largest network of caves in the world.

The Virtual Cave (www.goodearthgraphics.com/virtcave/ index.html). This amazing and well-organized Web site features a lot of great information about caves and cave formations as well as many beautiful photographs.

Index

Picture Credits

About the Author

Rachel Lynette has visited several show caves including Carlsbad Caverns, the Oregon Caves, and Lewis and Clark Caves in Montana. She has written seven other books for KidHaven Press, as well as dozens of articles on children and family life. She lives in the Seattle area in the Songaia Cohousing Community with her two children, David and Lucy; her dog, Jody; her cat, Cookie; and two playful rats. When she is not teaching or writing, she enjoys spending time with her family and friends, traveling, reading, drawing, and in-line skating.